The Naval & Military Press Ltd

Published by

The Naval & Military Press Ltd
Unit 5 Riverside, Brambleside
Bellbrook Industrial Estate
Uckfield, East Sussex
TN22 1QQ England

Tel: +44 (0)1825 749494

www.naval-military-press.com

In reprinting in facsimile from the original, any imperfections are inevitably reproduced and the quality may fall short of modern type and cartographic standards.

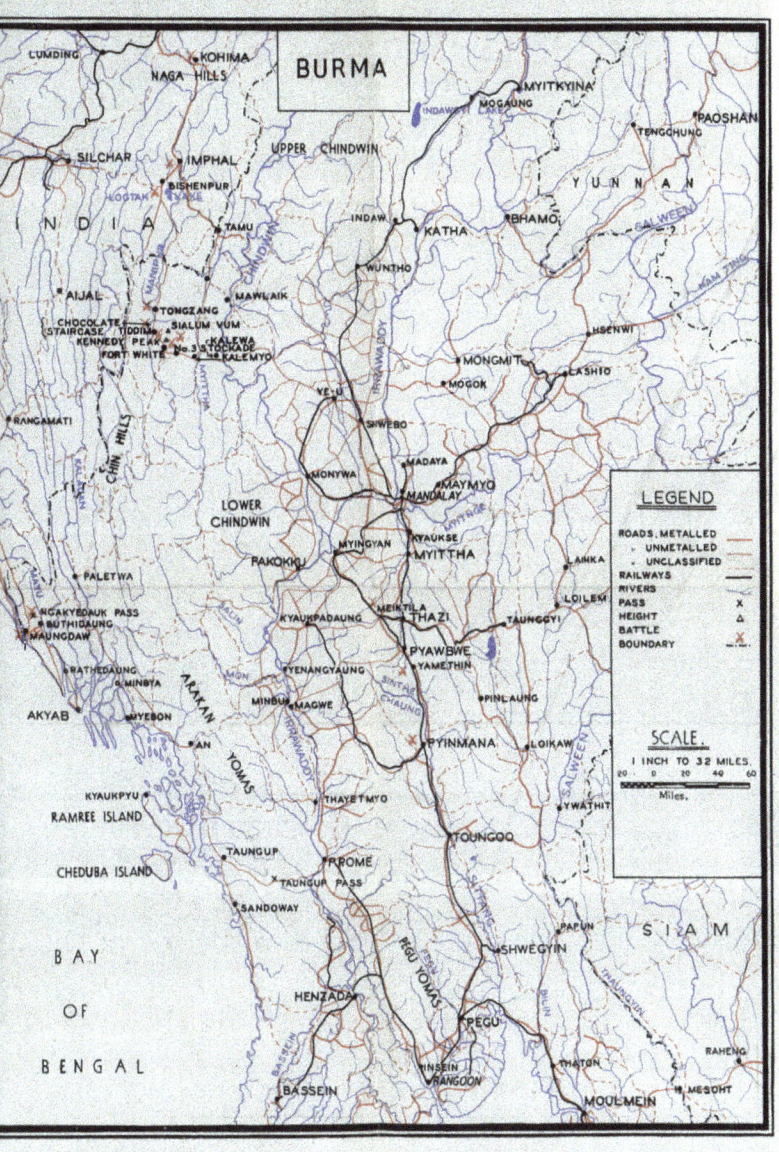

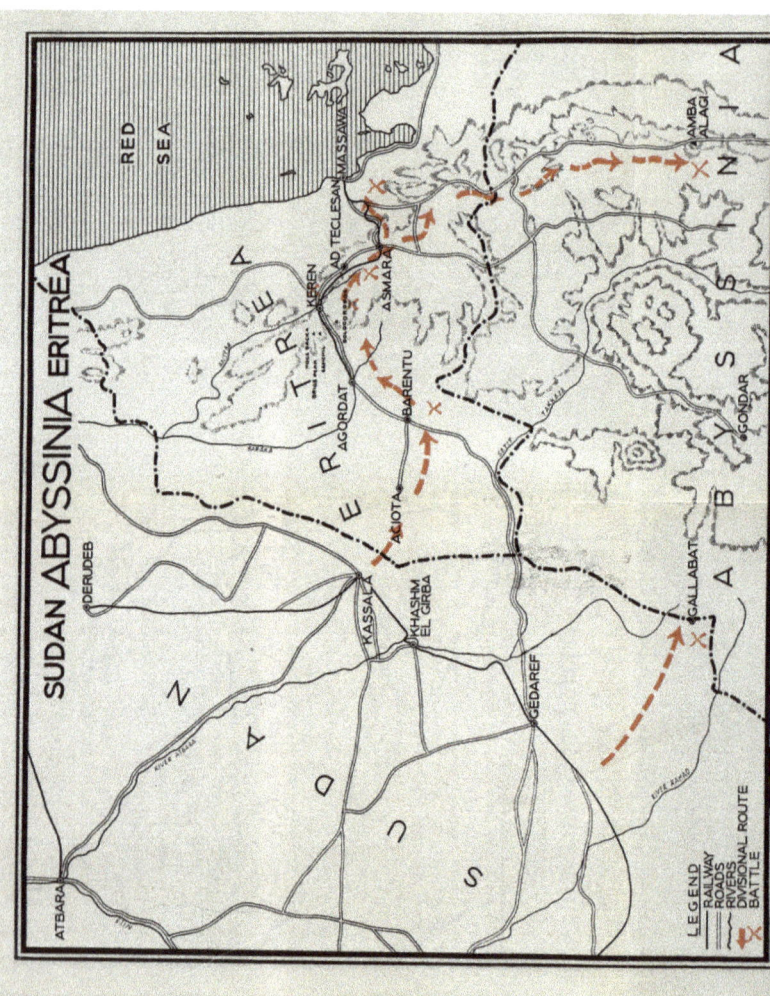

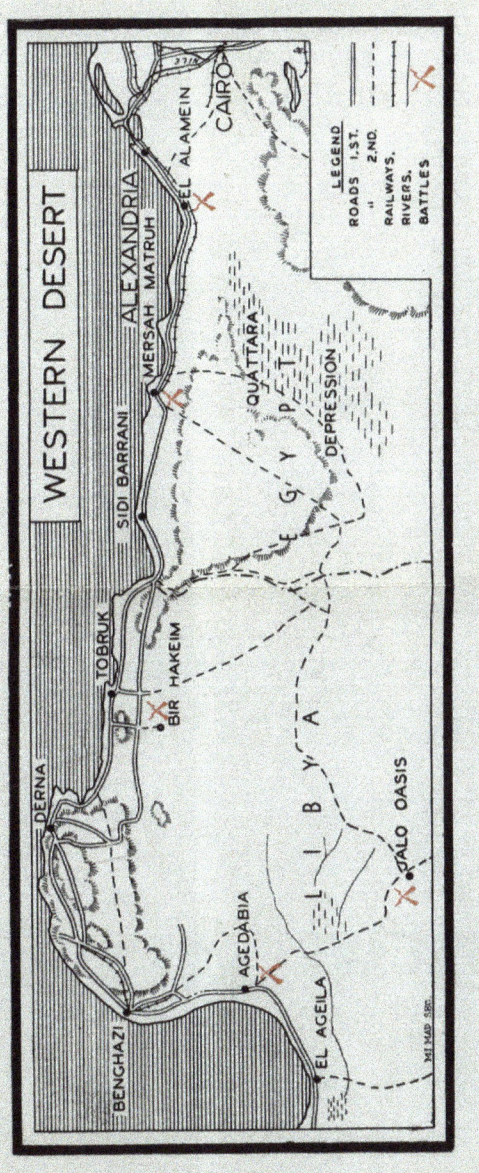

Lt.-Gen. SIR LEWIS HEATH, K.B.E., C.B., C.I.E., D.S.O., M.C., who commanded the 5th INDIAN DIVISION from July '40 to April '41.

★

Gen. SIR MOSLEY MAYNE, K.C.B., C.B.E., D.S.O., A.D.C., who commanded the 5th INDIAN DIVISION from April '41 to May '42.

★

Major-General (now Lt. Gen.) H. R. BRIGGS, C.B.E., D.S.O., who commanded the 5th INDIAN DIVISION from May '42 to July '44

★

Major-General G. C. EVANS, C.B.E., D.S.O., who commanded the 5th INDIAN DIVISION from July '44 until Sept. '44.

★

Major-Gen. D. F. W. WARREN, C. B. E., D.S.O., who commanded the 5th INDIAN DIVISION from Sept. '44 to Feb. '45.

★

Major-Gen. E.C. MANSERGH, C.B.E., M.C., the present commander of the 5th INDIAN DIVISION.

★

The Four V.Cs  of the 'Fifth'

Lance-Corporal J. P. Harman V.C., 4th Bn. the Queen's Own Royal West Kent Regt. while commanding a section within 50 yards of the enemy at Kohima, he twice went forward alone, and by shooting and bayoneting annihilated two enemy positions. On returning from his second exploit he received a burst of machine-gun fire in the side and was mortally wounded. (Posthumous).

Major P. SINGH BHAGAT, V.C., Royal Bombay Sappers and Miners. For outstanding bravery in Abyssinia.

Jem. ABDUL HAFIZ, V.C., 9th Jat Regt. For unsurpassed heroism when attacking the enemy near Imphal. Posthumous.

Sub. SARUP SINGH, V.C., 1st Punjab Regt. F gallantry while leadi an attack near Tiddi Posthumous.

THE "FIGHTING FIFTH"

ALMOST continuously in action, or in transit by land, sea and air from one battlefield to another during five years of war, the 5 Ind. Div. is one of the most travelled formations of the Empire's armies and has justly earned its title, "The Fighting Fifth".

From the wilderness of rocky peaks in Abyssinia, over thousands of miles of burning sands in North Africa, Iraq and Persia to the steaming jungles of Burma, the Division played a leading part in the defeat of the Italians, the Germans and the Japanese; crowning its epic campaigns with the occupation of Singapore on the surrender in the East.

At one time or another during the long war years, most of the finest units of the Indian Army served with, or fought alongside, the 5 Ind. Div. and the divisional sign—a ball of fire on a black background—was honoured wherever fighting men foregathered, just as it was feared by the Empire's enemies.

During the successive tides of battle, honours and awards were heaped on the soldiers of the "Fighting Fifth" for countless acts of bravery. Early in the Division's history at Gondar, Abyssinia, in January '41, 2nd/Lt. (now Major) Premindra Singh Bhagat, Royal Bombay Sappers and Miners, won the Indian Army's first Victoria Cross of the war. Later, in the Indo-Burma battles against the Japanese, more than 200 decorations were awarded to officers and men in the Division's Indian and British units, including three more V.C's.—won by L/Cpl. J. P. Harman, of the Royal West Kents, Jemadar Abdul Hafiz, of the 9th Jats, and Jemadar Ram Sarup Singh, 1st Punjab Regiment.

PART I. The Middle East.

FORMED in India in 1939, under the command of Major-Gen. L. M. Heath, C.B., C.I.E., D.S.O., M.C. (Now Lieut.-Gen. Sir Lewis Heath), the Division left for the Middle East in the summer of 1940 where one Brigade joined the 4 Ind. Div. and the two remaining Brigades were reformed to include three British battalions in the Sudan, which became its sphere of action.

Before the arrival of the Fifth in the Sudan the anxieties of the Kaid must have been very considerable and even after its arrival anxiety was not removed, for all along the frontier, wherever our forces faced each other, the enemy had at least a three to one advantage.

The greatest threat was from the direction of the Kassala triangle, from which direction it would have been quite possible for the enemy to have held our force, consisting of one Brigade group at the Atbara bridgehead and to have advanced down the right bank of the Atbara on to the town of that name, which was our main base.

A card in the hands of the Kaid, which could not be played until the Fifth gave an opening lead, was the patriot movement fostered by what was known as the " Rackets Department " and led in the interior of Abyssinia by half a dozen adventurous British officers.

It was primarily to give an impetus to this movement that the operation for the capture of Gallabat was staged. This operation gave an immense fillip to the patriots, and the Italians, fearing a rising on the Gallabat-Gondar line, trebled their forces in that area at the expense of centrally situated reserves and even withdrew internal security troops from other parts of the country. This operation was carried out by a Brigade commanded by Brigadier W. J. Slim, later to become world-famous as Gen. Sir William Slim, Commander of the Allied Land Forces, S.E.A. The clash with the Italians at Gallabat was also the battle baptism of the Division.

Plans were then made for the capture of the Kassala triangle to remove the most serious threat to the Sudan and to be the preliminary for an ambitious offensive, for which the troops in the Sudan were reinforced by the 4 Ind. Div., one Medium Battery of 6" Hows. and one squadron of infantry tanks. On 19th January 1941, the Fifth went into full scale action, beginning the offensive which was to result in the capture of Eritrea ; but before the blow fell, the Italians evacuated not only Kassala, but also had withdrawn from the outlying positions at Gulsa, Gamel and Gidda.

As it was thought that the enemy had withdrawn no further than the line Sabderat-Tessenei, a Brigade group, less one battalion which had already been committed at Abugamel, was sent on a wide flanking movement to cut

GALLABAT—Carriers of the 3/18th ROYAL GARHWAL RIFLES mopping-up in the town after fierce hand to hand fighting.

off all troops in the Tessenei area. The objectives next allotted to the 4 and 5 Ind. Divs. were respectively Agoradat and Barentu. The 5 Ind. Div., 10 Brigade leading, advanced unopposed and reached Aiciota on 21 January. After some stiff fighting around Barentu gorge, the Italians evacuated all their positions and Barentu was entered on the morning of 2nd February.

As far as the 5 Ind. Div. was concerned this phase ended the operation.

As all attempts to find an alternative approach to Asmara had failed, by the third week in February the Fifth were

THE WEST YORKS—*Smashed forward along a knife-edged ridge to storm and capture Fort Dologorodoc, subsequently resisting all counter-attacks.*

faced with the necessity of having to storm and capture Keren, where the Italians were entrenched in what they believed to be impregnable positions.

Demonstrating the prowess and teamwork of Indian and British troops working together within a formation, the infantry time and again assaulted the dizzy heights and, after much savage fighting, reduced them. During this prodigious feat of arms, every feature, scaled under a hail of fire, was named after the regiments which performed outstanding feats of bravery upon them. Among the names were Cameron Ridge, Rajputana Ridge and Sikh Spur.

KEREN - Mules and men of the R.I.A.S.C. bring up food, ammunition and stores for the forward troops, during the battle for Keren.

Keren fell on March 27th and, within the next fortnight, Asmara and Massawa were also in the bag; while the Fifth pushed on towards the mountain fortress of Amba Alagi, where the Italian forces were to make their last desperate stand in this tremendous natural stronghold.

Undaunted, the men of the Fifth and their fighting comrades stormed the sheer walls of rock with amazing dash and courage to win their crowning triumph, when the Italian Viceroy and Commander-in-Chief, the Duke of Aosta, surrendered personally to Major-Gen. A. G. O. M. Mayne (later General Sir Mosley Mayne), who was then

The 5th DIVISION entered MASSAWA to the sound of loud explosions coming from the harbour. A horrid mess had been made of the quays.

commanding the Fifth Indian Division. The fortress fell on 15 May, 1941.

By now the "Fighting Fifth" had advanced more than 500 miles across deserts, up mountains, in burning heat and drenching rain and throughout had carried no tentage. They had fought in the titanic struggle at Keren, won the battles of Barentu, Ad Teclesan and Massawa and had taken prisoners more than twice their own number.

In all these triumphs, the famous British battalions and the splendid British gunners within the Division had borne their share and officers and men of the Indian Army were the

Above: *THE ADVANCE ON AMBA ALAGI — A Bren-gun section of the Royal Frontier Force Rifles gives covering fire during the final attack.*

★

Right: *The Duke of Aosta, accompanied by Maj-Gen. A. G. O. M. Mayne (now Gen. Sir Mosley Mayne) come down from Amba Alagi.*

first to pay tribute to the part played by their British Army comrades.

In a farewell message to the "Fighting Fifth" Major-Gen. L. M. Heath recorded his appreciation of their soldierly qualities by his "Order of the Day" dated 10th April, 1941, as follows:

ORDER OF THE DAY
By
MAJOR-GENERAL L. M. HEATH, C.B., C.I.E., D.S.O., M.C., COMMANDER, 5TH INDIAN DIVISION.

10th April, 1941.

On relinquishing command of the 5th Ind. Div., I desire to place on record my very high appreciation of the soldierly qualities displayed by my troops and by those who have supported them and maintained them.

Since the offensive commenced in mid January, the Division has been victorious in every action that has been fought.

The first phase concluded with the occupation of BARENTU and WAHNI, the fighting for which was hard.

The second phase opened on the 15th March, after a period of stern training for the even more formidable tasks which lay ahead. It was in this training period that the foundation for success was laid.

None but seasoned, fit and well-disciplined troops, magnificently led, could have hoped to achieve success.

The capture of the DOLOGORODOC position and the FORT itself and the stubborn and successful resistance, over a period of ten days, to all attempts to retake it, must for all time rank high in Military annals. Seldom can troops have been called upon to show greater tenacity and endurance; exposed to intense and accurate fire of every description, the troops themselves, assisted by the Cypriot Mule Corps, carried many tons of ammunition, water and supplies up the precipitous fire-swept slopes. For ten days the enemy battered himself in his abortive, though most determined, counter-attacks to retake the position. During this stern period, the way was well prepared for exploitation of our gain, and that exploitation was carried out so courageously and with such dash and determination that the enemy army defending KEREN was shattered.

For the defence of the Capital of Eritrea he was compelled to bring forward all his available reserves. Though the defenders were throughout favoured by terrain, they failed to withstand our successive and vigorous onslaughts. Within space of fifteen days the Italian Eritrean Army which, for several weeks had fought so stubbornly, was overwhelmed and ASMARA was entered on the 1st April, 1941. Eight days later, troops of the Division in co-operation with troops of the 4th Indian Division, the Sudan Defence Force and the French Foreign Legion captured the formidable defences of MASSAWA. In achieving this success, The Royal Tank Regiment rendered most conspicuous service.

The infantry has borne the brunt of the fighting and has sustained the majority of the casualties. The infantryman, however, will be the first to praise the unstinted and skilful support afforded by the other arms of the Service ; all have had to work at top pressure and their efforts have been tireless : Gunners, Signals, Transport, Supply, Ordnance, Medical and the Clerical establishments, all have displayed superlative devotion to duty.

In addition, special tribute must firstly be paid to the Sapper and Miner Companies who worked with almost superhuman energy, quite undaunted by shot or shell, in their task of clearing the several demolitions encountered during our advances, and secondly to the Mobile Troops who co-operated : the Sudan Defence Force Motor Machine Gun Companies and Light Artillery, and the Central India Horse who together enabled success to be confirmed.

Without the gallant and ever generous co-operation of the Royal Air Force not only could victory not have been achieved but the operations could not have been undertaken : to the R.A.F. all will desire to join me in offering extreme appreciation and gratitude.

For the services which have been rendered, praise from the highest quarters has been received and that these tributes be not forgotten they are herein placed on record.

In bidding you farewell, I hereby desire to thank each individual soldier and airman for the part he has played in contributing to the victories of the Division under my command in Eritrea. May your victorious career continue.

(Sd.) **L. M. HEATH,**
Major-General, Commander, 5 Ind. Div.

On 18th November '41, we started our offensive in the Western Desert and here again men of the 5 Ind. Div. were to play a prominent part.

Transferred to the desert after a brief respite, troops of the Fifth created a diversion from Giarabub towards the

INTO THE CAULDRON—*British and Indian troops of 10th Ind. Inf. Bde. dash side by side into attack, fighting a desperate and gallant action.*

Jalo Oasis, while the 4 Ind. Div. attacked the strongly fortified enemy positions in Libyan Omar. A Brigade of the Fifth, operating from Giarabub, made a remarkable cross-desert dash of about 300 miles, reached and captured Jalo and took some 700 prisoners.

After a short rest, the Indian column in Jalo sallied forth about the middle of December, and, after a hazardous march took up positions 35 miles south of Agedabia. When the Germans started their counter offensive on 21st January 1942, the Fifth fought a rearguard action. To begin with, it was a battle of armour versus armour and the infantry had little chance to play a decisive part.

Following our heavy tank losses in June, however, troops of the Fifth fought a series of heroic rearguard actions, as Rommel's reinforced panzers swept back to Mersa Matruh. Repeatedly coming up against German armour, they suffered severe losses; but took heavy toll of the enemy.

After they had been taken out of the line to re-form and reorganise, the Fifth went into action again in time to play an important part in the defensive battle of El Alamein. For three months the ding-dong struggle went on at the Ruweisat Ridge and the Division, avenging some of its earlier misfortunes, took 2,000 prisoners in its last action in the North African theatre.

The Division was then moved to Iraq and Persia in support of Allied efforts to establish law and order after German influence had been eradicated in a campaign in which the 10 Ind. Div. had distinguished itself.

It was vital to the Allies that Persia and Iraq be kept safe from the possibility of the enemy making full use of his thrust across the Caspian. 5 Ind. Div. was formed into an Armoured Division of 7 Armoured Brigade (Desert Rats) and two Infantry Brigades. It was trained as a strong G.H.Q. reserve in the event of German penetration into either country, to protect the air line to India, the land supply route to Russia, and the oilfields.

This, however, was not the last change in store, for the Division was ordered to prepare for war against the Japanese. Thus, within a year, from May, 1942 to May, 1943, the Fifth had three roles—those of an Infantry Division for desert warfare, an Armoured Division, and, finally a division for jungle warfare.

PART II. Burma.

JUNE, 1943, saw the Division back in India.

In November the Division was in action again—this time against the Japanese in the Arakan, on the Burma front. After the Division had driven the Japanese out of Maungdaw the enemy launched their full scale offensive and in February, 1944, the 7 Ind. Div. found themselves cut off.

The Fifth came to the rescue. With Japs all along its lines of communications these veterans swept aside all opposition and after much bloody fighting in the notorious Ngakyedauk Pass re-opened it and relieved the 7 Ind. Div. who with 9th Bn. of 5 Div. were holding out in their famous "Admin" box in which the 2nd Bn. West Yorkshire Regt. of the 5th Indian Division played an outstanding part.

The Japanese had dug themselves in on jungle-clad hills dominating the Pass, which they held, closing it to the supply columns of the 7 Ind. Div. for 16 days until British tanks and Indian infantry of the 5 Ind. Div. pushed through from the western end of the pass and the Seventh sent out men from a Scottish Regiment to link up with them.

On the morning of 23rd February a British Officer, who had led Punjabi and Rajput fighters in a two-day jungle march to the rear of the enemy hill bunkers and had stormed and cleared them, came out of the jungle to greet a Scottish soldier of the 7 Ind. Div.

Commanding the 5 Ind. Div. at that time was Major-General H. R. Briggs, D.S.O.

The record of achievements of the 5 Ind. Div. during this period proved the excellent fighting quality of its men and, as soon as the Ngakyedauk Pass was clear and the Japanese had been pushed down south, the Fifth started on an offensive role. Much of the initial slogging and spade work, which finally led to the opening of the Maungdaw-Buthidaung tunnel road, was done by this Division before it was suddenly summoned from the Arakan scene.

Failing to break through in the Arakan, the Japanese had turned their attention to the Manipur front and began their attempted thrust into India. Soon the Fourteenth Army troops, battling fiercely to hold the Jap hordes, desperately needed reinforcements.

Where could reserves best be spared? Quick conferences were held and it was decided that the "Fighting Fifth" should be switched from the Arakan. First thoughts were to use road and rail. "Faster, faster" came the order and so the daring decision was taken to fly the 5 Ind. Div. from its old battleground to the new one amid the mountains and jungles of Manipur.

During ten hectic days in mid-March, troops, guns, jeeps and mules of the "Fighting Fifth" were loaded into transports and flown to Imphal, nearly 400 miles away.

Troops, guns, jeeps and mules of the "Fighting Fifth" were loaded into Dakotas and flown to IMPHAL nearly 400 miles away.

By overland transport such a move would have taken five to six weeks. It marked a new record; for, probably, never before has a formation of such size, quite untrained as airborne troops, been lifted bodily to places so far apart straight out of one battle into another.

Within a few days they had brought the Japanese to battle, the beginning of a series of actions that were to turn the scale against the enemy and prove that the much vaunted " March on Delhi " was no more than a myth. The seasoned soldiers of the " Fighting Fifth "—Dogras, Jats, Punjabis, West Yorks and Suffolks scored conspicuous successes, the earliest being the evacuation of a valuable ordnance dump, which was under fire from a strong enemy force ten miles north of Imphal and hundreds of Japanese fell before the veterans of Eritrea, Abyssinia and the Western desert.

Two V.Cs were won by members of the 5 Ind. Div. in the grim fighting at this period. On 5th April a Brigade of the Fifth moved up the Manipur Road to Kohima, where the Royal West Kents were able to beat the enemy for possession of the last ridge, which served as a base for the Kohima "inner" garrison. They held this ridge against overwhelming odds for 13 days, before Rajputs and Punjabis, who had also been isolated on another height a mile to the north fought through to their aid.

It was at Kohima that L/Cpl. J. P. Harman, Royal West Kents, won his posthumous V.C., and, when the Division was given the task of clearing the Imphal-Kohima Road, Jemadar Abdul Hafiz, of the 9th Jat Regiment, became the first Muslim to win a Victoria Cross in the war. He led his men with such ferocity that the Japanese fled from their position. Mortally wounded, he called on his party to re-organise, while he provided covering fire. He was too weak to pull the trigger, but his men swept on to victory.

The Japanese "March on Delhi" army was demoralised and reduced; but in spite of the monsoon season, hitherto considered impossible campaigning weather, the 14th Army were to give them no respite. After three months' siege around Imphal, the Kohima road was reopened with the meeting of the 2nd British and 5th Indian Divisions in June.

Later, two 14th Army spearheads plus the 11th East African Division and the 5 Ind. Div. had battered the enemy back from the Imphal Plain—down the Tamu road,

TROL OF THE 1/1st PUNJAB REGT. CLEAR AND CAPTURE A VILLAGE
EMYO WHICH WAS BEING USED BY THE JAPANESE AS A PATROL BASE.

All that remained of shell-shattered TIDDIM when the 5th Indian Division captured it after weeks of intense air and artillery bombardment.

through the treacherous Kabaw valley and the precipitous Tiddim road through the Chin hills—to meet victoriously in the valley of the Chindwin, around Kalemyo.

From the time when, locked in a bitter struggle, British and Indian troops held the Japanese at Bishenpur, the enemy gave way slowly and unwillingly along the road back to Tiddim and Kennedy Peak. At first the advance was slow, for the Japanese were organised in some force in the valley mouth, where the road debouches into the Imphal plain.

Repeated air strikes, backed up by spectacular tank attacks, weakened the enemy; and steadily the tide of battle rolled back to the Burma border. As the road became more precipitous, tanks and artillery were winched up hillsides, climbing thickly wooded slopes of 30 degrees, so that the guns could be brought to bear on Japanese positions.

As they retreated, the enemy steadily carried out demolitions, and in one stretch of 56 miles a company of the Royal Bombay Sappers and Miners had to build no less than 2,000-ft. of bridging of various types. Several times the infantry had to push back the enemy to permit the indispensable bulldozers to fill in huge craters to allow tanks to continue the advance.

First to recross the Burma border were men of the West Yorks who, working in patrol ahead of the 5 Ind. Div., covered 50 miles of hilly jungle in five days. But progress for the remainder was slow; an unending series of exposed corners, which the enemy were able to cover with their artillery, provided natural advantages to the retreating Japanese, and seriously threatened to delay the advance of the main body.

A solution was found in wide patrol detours using mule transport where possible, through almost endless elephant grass and thick jungle clustering the dizzy hillsides, to cut the enemy's rear line of communications.

These tactics culminated in a brilliant march by 123 Brigade commanded by Brigadier E. J. Denholm Young, D.S.O. and bar, which took the enemy completely by surprise.

While the main body of the Division pushed slowly on towards the Manipur river struggling every yard of the way to get the guns, tanks and vehicles safely through an endless series of avalanches along the precipitous road, which had been turned into a river of mud for mile after

A mortar detachment of the 1/17th DOGRAS pound Jap positions near the TONGZANG Road Block.

mile, 123 Brigade retraced their steps, and crossed the Manipur river at a narrow point higher up.

Making an 80 miles detour through dense jungle and over treacherously steep terrain, where often even the mules were unable to proceed without assistance, the Brigade emerged from the jungle and swooped on Tongzang, a Chin district centre and first place of any size between Imphal and Tiddim. They took the enemy completely by surprise, killed the majority of the defenders and captured eleven guns all trained to cover our main crossing of the river.

In the wooded heights overlooking the Manipur river

the Japanese had established deadly artillery positions commanding the crossing, where, with the bridge wrecked, the river, swollen by the rains to a roaring spate, presented an almost impassable barrier to the main body of the Division, so long as the enemy held the opposite bank.

123 Brigade not only caused the Japs to abandon their positions, but won space to function as the Divisional spearhead within striking distance of Tiddim, the tiny village nestling in the 6,000 feet high shoulder of the Chin Hills.

Supplied largely by air, with only a few mules for transport, the column moved along tracks that often had to be cut by the troops themselves and, to reach their objective climbed seven mountain ranges of 5,000 feet and two of 6,000 ft. struggling days on end along almost vertical mountain sides.

Punjabis were the first to hit a leading enemy position on this detour march. They quickly took up positions and held the road, while others dashed to attack a village, which was being used by the enemy as a patrol base. Surprised by this onslaught from the jungle-clad hills, the Japs fled.

For the attack on Tongzang, road blocks were put down by Indian troops on both sides of the Japanese stronghold. Then, with the enemy trapped, the Punjabis swept into the village, shouting their war cries, creating havoc. Some of the enemy, in a desperate attempt to retrieve their guns, tried to rush one of the road blocks, but were repulsed by Dogra infantry.

Several high features still remained between Tongzang and Tiddim and, despite the severe reverses they had suffered, the enemy stubbornly fell back from one strongpoint to

For weeks the 5th DIVISION were supplied by British and United States Flyers. Dakotas dropping supplies at TIDDIM.

another only after the most intense air and artillery pounding. Most famous was the Chocolate Staircase, the dark brown trail cut in the hillside, which wound several thousand feet up in a devastating series of hairpin bends from the bed of the Beltang Lui, tributary of the Manipur river.

The Japanese were dislodged from this natural fortress by Dogra infantry, who, after crossing swollen waters of the Beltang Lui under cover of darkness, climbed through the thick undergrowth up the steep hillside and straddled the road several miles up, forcing the enemy to withdraw to the heights around hill 160, ten miles further on.

The Division at this stage was commanded by Maj.-Gen. D. F. W. Warren, C.B.E., D.S.O.

Meanwhile, with tanks, artillery, vehicles and animal transport finally brought safely across the swiftly flowing Manipur river, many miles behind the forward infantry, it was decided to abandon the road from Imphal and close it behind the Division, which henceforth was to rely on air drops for all supplies, including 25 pdr. ammunition.

Some "experts" believed that it was only possible to supply such a large formation by air for three days; but for weeks British and United States flyers steadily dropped food, ammunition and clothing, medical supplies, signal equipment and even Jeep engines—in fact everything the Division needed to continue its non-stop chase of the Japanese.

Before the assault on Hill 160 and the last heights before Tiddim, the tanks were brought forward to the foot of Chocolate Staircase and hidden overnight. Then at dawn, while aircraft circled overhead to drown the noise of the engines of the armoured vehicles, the tanks made the ascent through low cloud, which covered their progress up the tortuous track. When the tanks emerged through the mists on the 6,000 ft. summit, British and Indian troops were amazed that they had been able to make the climb; but they were not so surprised as the Japanese, when the tanks went into action in the final thrust for Tiddim.

The heights and ridges before Tiddim were only cleared after two weeks of the most intense air and artillery pounding of the campaign and, without the splendid co-operation of the Air Force, the whole action would have been most costly in time and casualties to the Indian infantry, who

Hurri-bomber strike on Kennedy Peak historic milestone of the climax of the " Battle of the Peaks ".

took the township. As a mark of their appreciation of the part played by the airmen, the following signal was sent to 221 Group of the R.A.F. from the 1/17 Dogras : " The 1st Dogras wish to congratulate the R.A.F. on their successful liberation of Tiddim and consider it an honour to have co-operated."

Punjabis also played a great part in the capture of the township, although they did not take part in the frontal assault. Two battalions of these troops (3/2 and 2/1 Punjabs) crossed the Beltang Lui at the foot of the Chocolate Staircase, and swept in a wide left hook through most difficult terrain to the Japs' rear, behind Tiddim.

They thus helped the Dogra infantry in their task of storming the staircase and capturing the township, while they pushed on to appear on the road nine miles beyond Tiddim, ready to strike at the towering heights of Kennedy Peak (8,800-ft.). Yet another battalion (1/1 Punjab) made an even wider outflanking movement, repeating the process even farther behind the Japanese on whom they swooped at Stockade Three.

They made marches of more than five weeks over some of the steepest mountain ranges in the Chin territory and were among the most arduous made by any troops down the Tiddim road and beyond. Often the men had to crawl hand over hand up steep cliffs and along narrow ledges, so that even the mules—many of which had been campaigning for nearly four years—became panic-stricken and slipped over the edge.

In one of these flanking movements the 2/1 Punjab captured the strong enemy position at Sialum Vum, overlooking the road from Tiddim to Kennedy Peak and Fort White and sat there with their mountain guns continually harrassing the enemy's line of communication for nearly four weeks—miles behind the Japanese forward troops; and with a baffled Japanese company positioned only 500 yards away on the ridge below them.

Here, on 25th October, 1944, Subedar Ram Sarup Singh (2/1 Punjab) won the Victoria Cross. Before the action, in which he led repeated bayonet charges to dislodge the Japanese from their bunkers, the Subedar said to his Company commander: "Sahib, either the Jap or myself die today." When, mortally wounded by Machine-gun fire which he had

Left: *Gurkha Signal N... on duty during the ba... for Kennedy Peak.*

Right: *That was FO... WHITE—Japanese stro... hold in the Chin H...*

drawn on himself, he called with his dying breath to his platoon havildar. "I am dying, but you carry on and finish the devils."

In the battle of the peaks dominating the Fort White road winding down to the open country around Kalemyo, Kennedy Peak was the chief obstacle, where the Japs were strongly ensconced in old fortified positions. As a prelude to this final phase of the campaign, tanks and guns were moved by moonlight to forward positions, creeping along the narrowest of ridges with dizzy drops of many thousands of feet on either side while British gunners gave support to the Indian infantry from fantastic positions on the sheer mountain sides, where their guns had been lowered by ropes.

Kennedy Peak fell to the Fighting Fifth when crack Punjab infantry raced up the heights from the east to meet Mahommedans and Dogra Rajputs of the Jammu and Kashmir State Force, who had fought up the heights from the west.

Encountering little serious opposition the Division then pushed on through Fort White and Stockade Three to Kalemyo and linked up with the 11th East African Division.

Having fought continuously for 14 months, the Fifth then returned to Assam and rested for two months before entering Burma again in March 1945, travelling more than 1,000 miles by road through Imphal, Kalewa, Monywa, Myitche and Meiktila.

It was the capture of Meiktila in March (1945), which made possible the rapid advance on Rangoon from the north and in this battle men of the 5 Ind. Div. played a prominent part.

9 Brigade flew to Meiktila between 15th and 18th March, just as the Japanese were preparing their big counter-attack on the town, which had been captured by the 17 Ind. Div. a fortnight before.

Daringly planned, the fly-in to the airstrip around which Japanese snipers were very active, was carried out by United States Commando pilots, their planes landing their cargoes in four minutes. Indian troops of the 14th Punjab Regt., the Jammu and Kashmir Infantry, Bombay Sappers and Miners and the renowned West Yorks, together with a Brigade head quarters, flew into 14th Army's advanced citadel in this manner.

In the rush towards Pegu, the same Brigade was flown several days march southward to land on a forward strip a few days before the fall of Rangoon.

They took over the drive south towards Rangoon from 17 Ind. Div. on 10th April 1945 at Pyawbwe, 23 air miles south of Meiktila. The Division was now under the command of Major-General E. C. Mansergh, C.B.E., M.C., who had succeeded Major-General D. F. W. Warren, C.B.E., D.S.O., who was killed in an air accident in February.

Less than three weeks later when they again handed over to the 17 Ind. Div. the Fifth had swept forward 180 miles after several stiff actions. At Yamethin, 12 miles south of Pyawbwe, the armoured column went through without interference; but the Japanese returned to the town from the east, and the leading infantry of the division had a tough two days fight before the place was cleared. In this action a battalion of the York and Lancaster regiment—new to Burma and to the Division—fought with great courage.

Further on, the same leading Brigade—the victors of Tongzang and Tiddim—in a masterly manoeuvre drove the enemy from a hill feature known as Shwemyo Bluff dominating the road to Rangoon, secured a bridgehead across the Sinthe Chaung and pushed on south.

At Pyinmana, 161 Brigade was left to mop up the Japanese garrison, which made a stubborn effort to stem the advance, while the main body of the Fifth by-passed the town following a diversion built by the sappers in enemy country ahead of the flying columns. The advance was then speeded up towards Toungoo and in one day the division covered 30 miles.

By April 26, when the Division was only about 130 miles from Rangoon, the lead was once more given to troops of 17 Ind. Div. and from that time until the Division embarked for the occupation of Malaya, the Division's time was largely taken with mopping up the very considerable bands of Japanese, which had been left behind in the whirlwind advance and in cutting the enemy's escape route to the east.

Adding fresh lustre to their brilliant record, the 5th Division was the first ashore at Singapore, on September 5, 1945, during the Allied re-occupation of Malaya. One of their tasks was the disarming and interrogating of 83,000 Japanese. In two months the Division was switched on to troubled Java, where the activities of the Indonesians were hindering the disarming and removal of the Japs and the safe evacuation of Allied internees. In the weeks which followed these troops found their hands full, restoring peace and order which continued to be violated by uncontrolled masses.

The odyssey of this great division is not yet ended. When they have fired their last shot the men of the Fifth will be conscious of a long road traversed and of a great job well and truly done.

A PHOTOGRAPHIC SURVEY OF THE MAIN BATTLE AREAS

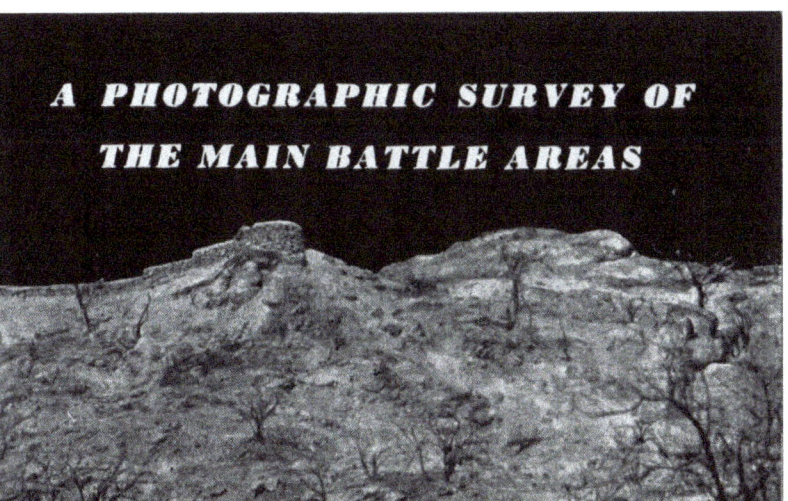

ERITREA. A close-up view of FORT DOLOGORODOC situated deep in the KEREN mountains, captured in March 1941.

ERITREA. A panorama from HOGS BACK showing the familiar features of BRIG'S PEAK, SANCHIL, DOLOGORODOC and CAMERON RIDGE.

Divisional BATTLE H.Q. near Keren under the shadow of Sanchil.

AMBA ALAGI and ELEPHANT MOUNTAIN. Burnt out Italian trucks in foreground.

WESTERN DESERT

JALO OASIS. Captured on 25th Nov. 1941 by 'E' Force. Photograph shows infantry attacking through gaps in wire made by carriers.

ARAKAN, BURMA

YAKYEDAUK PASS showing one of the countless hair-pin bends.

THE TUNNELS. Shattered entrance of the tunnel on the Buthidaung Road.

DOHAZARI AIRFIELD. With the sudden Japanese threat to Imphal, the whole division was transported by air to meet the emergency.

IMPHAL. Infantry of 123 Brigade and tanks move up before an attack.

KOHIMA. All that was left of the District Commissioner's bungalow.

BISHENPUR ROAD. Ambulance convoy stops while sappers repair damage.

BURMA. Troops of the DIVISION rest on the India-Burma border.

MANIPUR RIVER with the rough Tiddim road winding beside it.

BELTANG LUI. Destroyed bridge over the river at the foot of the "Chocolate Staircase".

AIR SUPPLY TO TIDDIM ROAD. A Dakota swoops in and drops supplies.

A BURMA BATTLEFIELD. A Panoramic view of the mountain ranges surrounding TIDDIM, showing the rugged country over which the troops fought.

KENNEDY PEAK, high in the Chin Hills. Troops move up to consolidate.

SYMBOL OF VICTORY. The flag raised at Fort White.

KALEMYO ROAD. Mud did not stop this truck.

OFFICERS of the 11th East African and 5th Divisions meet beyond Kalemyo.

INTHE. Under cover of an artillery concentration, a company of infantry are seen assaulting the village at the foot of the ridge.

SINGAPORE

SINGAPORE REOCCUPIED. INDIAN troops land. Japanese Ps. O. W. are rounded up

Below: Supreme Allied Commander Lord LOUIS MOUNTBATTEN inspects Dogra Reg

LAST, BUT NOT LEAST

ARMOURED UNITS. Link-up, Imphal road.

GUNNERS manhandle 3.7 m.m., Imphal road.

SAPPERS. Pontoon bridge, Manipur River.

SIGNALS. Signalman slings line in jungle.

SUPPLIES. The mules go forward.

MEDICAL SERVICES. Examination of X-Ray.

Units which served with the 5th

INFANTRY

2nd Bn. Suffolk Regt., 2nd Bn. West Yorkshire Regt., 1st Bn. Worcestershire Regt., 4th Bn. Essex Regt., 4th Bn. Royal West Kent Regt., 2nd Bn. Highland Light Infantry., 1st Bn. Argyll and Sutherland Highlanders, 1/1 Punjab, 1/2 Punjab, 3/1 Punjab, 3/2 Punjab, 1/5 Mahrattas, 2/5 Mahrattas, 3/5 Mahrattas, 1/6 Rajputana Rifles, 4/6 Rajputana Rifles, 3/9 Jats, 3/10 Baluch, 4/10 Baluch, 3/12 Royal Frontier Force Regt., 6/13 Royal Frontier Force Rifles, 3/14 Punjab, 1/17 Dogras, 3/18 Royal Garhwal Rifles, 2/4 Gurkha Rifles.

CAVALRY

4 Royal Tank Regt., 46 Royal Tank Regt., Skinners Horse.

ARTILLERY

25 A.A. Regt. R.A., 390 Fd. Regt. R.A., 44 Fd. Regt. R.A., 1 Fd. Regt. R.A., 68 Med. Regt. R.A., 4 Fd. Regt. R.A., 28 Fd. Regt. R.A., 1 Lt. A.A. Regt. R.A., 149 A. Tk. Regt. R.A., 11 Fd. Regt. R.A., 56 A.A./A. Tk. Regt. R.A., 28 Jungle Fd. Regt. R.A., Lt. A. A. Bty. Sudan Regt., J. and K. Mtn. Bty., 30 Ind. Mtn. Regt. I.A.

ENGINEERS

44 Fd. Park Coy. S.M., Det 2 Bridging Sec. S.M., 20 Fd. Coy. S.M., 2 Fd. Coy. S.M., 18 Fd. Coy. S.M., 21 Fd. Coy. S.M., 4 Fd. Coy. S. M., 74 Fd. Coy. I.E.

SIGNALS

Main 5 Ind. Div. Sigs., Rear 5 Ind. Div. Sigs., 4 Fd. Regt. R.A. Sigs. Sec., 28 Jungle Fd. Regt. Sigs. Sec., 56 AA/A. Tk. Regt. Sigs. Sec., 30 Ind. Mtn. Regt. I.A. Sigs. Sec., 9, 123 and 161 Ind. Infry. Bde. Sigs. Sec.

Division between 1939 and 1945

ROYAL INDIAN ARMY SERVICE CORPS

14, 15, 29 and 233 M.T. Coy., 23, 60, 74 and 82 A.T. Coy., 7, 60, 61 and 62 I.C.I.S. Coy., 11 B.S.S., 20, 101 and 103 S.I.S., 100 and 104 S.P.S., 8 and 16 Cattle Supply Sec., 9, 10, 29, 238, 239 and 240 I.G.P.T. Coy., 10 Fd. Butchery, 10 Fd. Bakery, Jaipur Pony Coy.

MEDICAL SERVICES

21 Fd. Amb., 2 Fd. Amb., 4 X-Ray Unit, 170 Lt. Fd. Amb., 1 Anti-Malarial Unit, 3 C.C.S., 7 Fd. Hyg. Sec., 20 Fd. Amb., 10 Ind. Fd. Amb., 19 Ind. Staging Section, 14 Ind. Fd. Amb., 26 Ind. Fd. Amb., 75 Ind. Fd. Amb., 45 Ind. Fd. Amb., 2 Ind. Mob. Vet. Sec.

ELECTRICAL AND MECHANICAL ENGINEERS

16 W/Shop Sec., 41 W/Shop Sec., 4 W/Shop Sec., 40 W/Shop Sec., 28 W/Shop Sec., 36 W/Shop Sec., 44 W/Shop Sec., 39 W/Shop Sec., 37 W/Shop Sec., 38 W/Shop Sec., 17, 21, 22, 24, 25, 26, 112 and 113 Mob. Ord. W/Shop Coy., 9, 123 and 161 Ind. L. A.D. Type E., 5 Ind. Rec. Coy.

MISCELLANEOUS UNITS

15, 21, 22, 23, 24, 89 and 169 F.P.O., Div. Provost Unit, 565 F.S.S., 5 Pl. Burma Int. Corps, Fd. Accounts Section, 12 Ind. Salvage Unit, 5 Labour Coy.

ADDITIONAL UNITS

3 Bn. East African Corps, 2 and 4 M.M.G. Coy., Camel Corps, 1st French Spahis, 52 (M.E.) Commando, 6 M.M.G. Coy., Sudan Regt., 24 Ind. Mtn. Regt.

INDIAN DIVISIONS WON A FINE REPUTATION IN WORLD WAR TWO

Field Marshal Auchinleck, Commander-in-Chief of the British Indian Army from 1942, asserted that the British *"couldn't have come through both wars (World War I and II) if they hadn't had the British Indian Army"*. British Prime Minister Winston Churchill also paid tribute to *"the unsurpassed bravery of Indian soldiers and officers"*.

Between 1945 and 1947, the Director of Public Relations, War Department, Government of India, published a series of short publications covering the individual histories of the WWII Indian Divisions. They followed a consistent format, having between 44 and 48 pages within illustrated soft card covers. They have an average of 50 monochrome photographic illustrations, and each has a full colour centrespread depicting a scene from the Division's wartime operations (drawn by official war artists). They were printed at various presses in Bombay and New Delhi, and each contains at least one map.

As condensed histories they are useful – particularly those which relate to Divisions for which no other record was ever produced.

The British Indian Army during World War II began the war, in 1939, numbering just under 200,000 men. By the end of the war, it had become the largest volunteer army in history, rising to over 2.5 million men in August 1945. Serving in divisions of infantry, armour and a fledgling airborne force, they fought on three continents: in Africa, Europe and Asia.

This Army fought in Ethiopia against the Italian Army, in Egypt, Libya, Tunisia and Algeria against both the Italian and German Army and, after the Italian surrender, against the German Army in Italy. However, the bulk of the British Indian Army was committed to fighting the Japanese Army, first during the British defeats in Malaya and the retreat from Burma to the Indian border; later, after resting and refitting for the victorious advance back into Burma, as part of the largest British Empire army ever formed. These campaigns cost the lives of over 87,000 Indian service- men, while another 34,354 were wounded, and 67,340 became prisoners of war. Their valour was recognised with the award of some 4,000 decorations, and 18 members of the British Indian Army were awarded the Victoria Cross or the George Cross.

RED EAGLES
The Story of the 4th Indian Division
9781474537520

During the Second World War, the 4th Indian Division was in the vanguard of nine campaigns in the Mediterranean theatre, Egypt, Eritrea, Syria, Tunisia, Italy and Greece. The 4th Division captured 150,000 prisoners and suffered 25,000 casualties, more than the strength of a whole division. It won over 1,000 honours and awards, which included four Victoria Crosses and three George Crosses. Field Marshal Lord Wavell wrote: "The fame of this Division will surely go down as one of the greatest fighting formations in military history."

THE FIGHTING FIFTH
History of the 5th Indian Division
9781474537513

As described in much greater detail in Anthony Brett James's book 'The Ball of Fire', the division saw active service in East Africa, North Africa and Burma.

GOLDEN ARROW
The Story of the 7th Indian Division
9781474537506

The role of this division is also duplicated by a much larger work: the book by Brig. M. R. Roberts. However, this booklet gives a good account of Kohima and Imphal and the crossing of the Irrawaddy. In 1945, the division was flown into Siam, so becoming the first Allied formation to re-enter South East Asia.

ONE MORE RIVER
The Story of the 8th Indian Division
Biferno, Trigno, Sangro, Moro, Rapido, Arno, Senio, Santerno, Po, Adige

9781474537490

The 8th Indian Division started its overseas service in the Middle East in the garrisoning of Iraq and then the invasion of Persia to secure the oil fields of the area for the Allies, before moving to Italy in 1943. Landing at Taranto, it pushed up the length of the peninsula in a series of major battles: breaking the Sangro Line, forcing the Rapido and turning the defences at Cassino, breaking the stubborn German resistance at Monte Grande and, finally, forcing the Po River. It won four VCs, 26 DSOs and 149 MCs along the way. During the war the 8th Indian Division sustained casualties totalling 2,012 dead, 8,189 wounded and 749 missing.

BLACK CAT DIVISION
17th Indian Division

9781474537483

This formation was committed to Burma from the early days when the British were in full flight from the invading Japanese. It remained in Burma right through to the end, when the starving remnants of the Japanese Army were making their own desperate retreat.

TIGER HEAD
The Story of the 26th Indian Division
Arakan, Ragoon

9781474537452

This is a history of the division said later by the Japanese to have been the opponent which they most feared. The 26th held the Allied monsoon line in the Arakan during two such seasons, repulsing every attack launched against it. Later it made a series of leap-frog landings down the coast to clinch the issue in the Arakan. It was the first division to enter Ragoon, invading the city from the sea.

A HAPPY FAMILY
The Story of the Twentieth Indian Division, April 1942-August 1945

9781474537476

One of the few Indian divisions in the 14th Army trained specifically for the war in Burma. Raised in Bangalore in 1942, it commenced active operations in late 1943 and served from Imphal through to the end. It established the 14th Army's first brigade-head across the Chindwin and its second such brigade-head across the Irrawaddy. Its final task was to round up the Japanese in French Indochina.

THE TWENTY THIRD INDIAN DIVISION
"The Fighting Cock Division"
Burma, Malaya, Java

9781474537469

The Fighting Cock Division is well recorded in the book by Doulton. This book gives coverage of the heavy fighting at the Kohima Battle, the capture of Tamu, the reoccupation of Malaya in August 1945, and then its strange role on the island of Java – concurrently disarming the Japanese garrison, fighting the insurgent Indonesian nationalists, and caring for 65,000 former internees pending the arrival of a new Dutch administration.

TEHERAN TO TRIESTE
The Story Of The Tenth Indian Division

9781783317028

This History deals with the 10th Indian Div's exploits in Iraq (under Maj Gen "Bill" Slim) its role in the Libyan battles leading up to El Alamein, the following two years of garrison duties in Cyprus and Syria, and finally, its fighting services in the Italian campaign (from Ortona onwards).

THE STORY OF THE 25th INDIAN DIVSION
The Arakan Campaign
9781783317585

Formed in Southern India in August 1942 for defence of that area in case of Japanese invasion, the "Ace of Spades" Division had its baptism of fire in Arakan in February 1944. It served throughout the remainder of that campaign the climax being the battle of Tamandu. Its victorious fight for the Kangaw roadblock was considered by many to have been the fiercest battle of the entire Burma war, while its liberation of Akyab was the first convincing proof to the rest of the world that the tide had turned against the Japanese.

DAGGER DIVISION
The Story Of The 19th Indian Division
9781783317035

Raised in the late 1941, the 19th was the first "standard" Indian Division. Its troops were the first to breach the Japanese defence line in Burma and to raise the flag at Fort Dufferin. It crossed the Chindwin in November 1944, driving on to Mandalay and Ragoon during seven months of continuous fighting. The 19th's exploits are graphically described also in John Masters' personal memoir, *The Road Past Mandalay*.

www.ingramcontent.com/pod-product-compliance
Lightning Source LLC
Chambersburg PA
CBHW041928090426
42743CB00021B/3477